DON'T PASSOVER
EASTER

A NEW DEFENSE OF "EASTER" IN ACTS 12:4

Bryan C. Ross

DISPENSATIONAL
PUBLISHING HOUSE, INC.

Scriptures quoted as KJV are taken from the KING JAMES VERSION (KJV).

Printed in the United States of America
ISBN: 978-1-945774-44-7

Dispensational Publishing House, Inc.
220 Paseo del Pueblo Norte
Taos, NM 87571

www.dispensationalpublishing.com

Ordering Information: Quantity sales. Special discounts are available on quantity purchases by churches, associations, and others. For details, contact the publisher at the address above.

Orders by U.S. trade bookstores and wholesalers. Please contact the publisher:
Tel: (844) 321-4202

1 2 3 4 5 6 7 8 9 10

To my parents Steve and Jeanie Ross. Thank you for all your love and support over the years. Your faithful stand for the King James Bible, the Pauline Grace Message, and the word of God rightly divided has been an encouragement and blessing to many. Thank you for raising me in nurture and admonition of the Lord and for the courage to make hard decisions pertaining to my early academic development without which none of these books would have been possible.

Table of Contents

"And when he had apprehended him, he put him in prison, and delivered him to four quaternions of soldiers to keep him; intending after Easter to bring him forth to the people."

(Acts 12:4)

Introduction

The question of whether or not "Easter" is an accurate translation of the Greek word *pascha* in Acts 12:4 in the King James Bible (KJB) is, in many ways, emblematic of the common assumption among King James Bible believers that the preservation, transmission, and translation of the Holy Scriptures occurred with *verbatim identicality* of wording. Critics of the King James in general, and King James Only opponents specifically, have sought to use Acts 12:4 as a case in point to prove that the KJB is not inerrant. It is alleged that "Easter" is a mistranslation of the Greek word *pascha* and, therefore, constitutes an error in the KJB.

Defenders of the inerrancy of the KJB have sought to answer these critics by putting forth arguments for why "Easter" is not a mistake in Acts 12:4. These King James apologists assert that *pascha* could only have been correctly translated "Easter" given the context of Acts 12. So, according to these brethren not only is "Easter" not a mistake but the "Passover" would constitute of textual corruption. This small booklet seeks to look at both sides of this controversy with the goal of reaching a reasonable and factual conclusion. In order to accomplish this task, the present volume will consider the following points:

- The Standard King James Only defense of "Easter" in Acts 12:4

- Is "Easter" exclusively pagan?

- "Easter" in the English Bible: A brief look at the history of translation

- Scriptural exposition of Acts 12:4

- How Gipp got it so wrong?

- The Christian "Passover" view

- Concluding thoughts

In the end, it will be demonstrated that "Easter" in Acts 12:4 means "Passover" as in the Jewish feast day and is not a reference to a pagan spring festival or a Christian holiday, as has been commonly asserted by both critics and advocates of the KJB.

Why the Controversy?

The Greek word *pascha* occurs 29 times in 27 verses in the *Textus Receptus*, the Greek text supporting the KJB. Of these 29 occurrences of *pascha* in the New Testament, the King James translators rendered it as "Passover" 28 times and only in Acts 12:4 do the translators render the Greek word as "Easter" in English. This has opened the door for critics of the KJB, to assert that "Easter" is a translational error in Acts 12:4 and should have been rendered as "passover" in

English. Consequently, critics of the King James have repeatedly cited Acts 12:4 as an example of a translational error in the KJB. The logic of these critical scholars is fundamentally based upon the following two assumptions:

1. The Greek word *pascha* ALWAYS equals "Passover" in English. *Pascha* has NEVER been associated with "Easter" in English. This notion is demonstrated by pointing out that modern versions of the Bible translate *pascha* as "Passover" every time it occurs in the text, including in Acts 12:4.

2. Parties on both sides of the textual debate view "Easter" as being pagan in origin and etymology. This is partly why modern version advocates view "Easter" as a mistaken translation of *pascha*. Meanwhile, King James apologists admit that "Easter" is pagan and defend it accordingly in Acts 12:4 as the only appropriate rendering of *pascha* given the context.

In his book *The King James Only Controversy*, Dr. James R. White concisely sums up the argument of critical scholars as follows:

> "One might include the KJV's unusual rendering of Acts 12:4 as more of a mistranslation than an ambiguous rendering, and it would be hard to argue against that assertion, given the facts.
>
> The word that the KJV translates as "Easter" appears twenty-nine times in the New Testament. In each of the other twenty-eight instances the KJV translates the phrase as "the Passover." For example, John 19:14, "And it was the

preparation of the Passover, and about the sixth hour: and he saith unto Jews, Behold your King!" And there is no reason for confusion as to what Luke is referring to here, for the preceding verse said, "Then were the days of unleavened bread." The days of unleavened bread, of course were connected with the Passover celebration. Yet in this one place the AV contains the anachronistic [belonging to a period other than the one portrayed] term "Easter." Luke's reference to the days of "unleavened bread" makes it clear that he is referring to the Jewish holiday season, not to some pagan festival that did not become known by the specific term "Easter" for some time to come."[1]

In summary, the critical argument, put forward by James White views the word "Easter" in Acts 12:4 as a "mistranslation" i.e., a mistake. The word is an anachronistic term, or a word used out of its proper historical context, according to Dr. White. Therefore, on White's view, the Greek word *pascha* never meant "Easter" in English. Rather, it always meant "Passover". Mark well, however, that White does not dispute the King James only assertion that "Easter" is a reference to a pagan holiday. Instead he refutes the notion that Luke is speaking about a pagan holiday in Acts 12:4. This verse is routinely cited as a proof text against the notion of "perfect preservation" as it has been defined by most King James advocates as requiring *verbatim identicality* of wording. Many King James advocates insist that any translation that reads "Passover" in Acts 12:4 is a "corruption" because "Easter" is the only correct word given the context of Acts 12. And thus, we have the current controversy.

---

1   James R. White. *The King James Only Controversy: Can You Trust Modern Translations?*. Bethany House Publishers: Minneapolis, MN: 1995, 233.

The Standard King James Only
Defense of Easter in Acts 12:4

Believers in the inerrancy of the King James Bible have sought to defend the King James rendering of *pascha* in Acts 12:4 in an effort to rescue their enterprise for critical scrutiny. The classic example of a King James Only defense of "Easter" in Acts 12:4 can be found in Dr. Samuel C. Gipp's 1989 publication *The Answer Book*. As the title suggests, *The Answer Book* is written in a question-and-answer format in which Dr. Gipp seeks to answer some of the frequently asked questions regarding the classic King James Only position. The question and answer regarding "Easter" comprise the books second entry.

> "QUESTION: Isn't "Easter" in Acts 12:4 a mistranslation of the word "*pascha*" and should it be translated as "passover"?
>
> ANSWER: No, "*pascha*" is properly translated "Easter" in Acts 12:4 as the following explanation will show.
>
> Coming to the word "Easter" in God's Authorized Bible, they seize upon it imagining that they have found proof that the Bible is not perfect. Fortunately for lovers of the

word of God, they are wrong. Easter, as we know it, comes from the ancient pagan festival of Astarte. Also known as Ishtar (pronounced "Easter"). This festival has always been held late in the month of April. It was, in its original form, a celebration of the earth "regenerating" itself after the winter season. The festival involved a celebration of reproduction. For this reason the common symbols of Easter festivities were the rabbit (the same symbol as "Playboy" magazine), and the egg. Both are known for their reproductive abilities. At the center of attention was Astarte, the female deity. She is known in the Bible as the "queen of heaven" (Jer. 7:18; 44:17-25). She is the mother of Tammuz (Ezekiel 8:14) who was also her husband! These perverted rituals would take place at sunrise on Easter morning (Ez. 8:13-16). From the references in Jeremiah and Ezekiel, we can see that the true Easter has never had any association with Jesus Christ.

Problem: Even though the Jewish passover was held in mid-April (the fourteenth) and the pagan festival Easter was held later the same month, how do we know that Herod was referring to Easter in Acts 12:4 and not the Jewish passover? **If he was referring to the passover, the translation of "pascha" as "Easter" is incorrect. If he was indeed referring to the pagan holyday (holiday) Easter, then the King James Bible (1611) must truly be the very word and words of God for it is the only Bible in print today which has the correct reading."**[2]

In support of his answer, Gipp goes on to present the following explanation for why "Easter" is the only correct translation of *pascha* in Acts 12:4. Passover occurred on the 14th of the month—and no event after the 14th is EVER referred to as Passover according to: Exodus

---

2 Samuel C. Gipp. *The Answer Book: A Help Book for Christians*. Bible & Literature Missionary Foundation: Shelbyville, TN: 1989, 3-4.

12:13-18, Numbers 28:16-18, and Deuteronomy 16:1-8.[3] The Days of Unleavened Bread began on the 15th of the month the day after Passover. The Days of Unleavened Bread are ALWAYS after Passover and are NEVER referred to as Passover, according to Dr. Gipp.[4] Peter was arrested in Acts 12:4 during the Days of Unleavened Bread AFTER Passover.[5] Therefore, Herod could not possibly have been referring to Passover in Acts 12:4 because the next Passover was a year away.[6] Herod, being a pagan Roman worshiped the queen of heaven and had no reason to keep the Jewish Passover.[7] Consequently, Herod did not kill Peter during the Days of Unleavened Bread because he wanted to wait until later in the month after the passing of his own holiday i.e., "Easter."[8]

---

3 "On the 14th of April the lamb was killed. This is the passover. No event following the 14th is ever referred to as the passover." Ibid., 7.

4 "Whenever the passover was kept, it **always** preceded the feast of unleavened bread. . . On the morning of the 15th begins the days of unleavened bread, also known as the feast of unleavened bread.

It must also be noted that whenever the passover is mentioned in the New Testament, the reference is **always** to the meal, to be eaten on the night of April 14th **not** the entire week. The days of unleavened bread are NEVER referred to as the Passover. (It must be remembered that the angel of the Lord passed over Egypt on **one** night, **not** seven nights in a row." Ibid., 6-7.

5 "Verse 3 shows that Peter was arrested during the days of unleavened bread (April 15-2 1). The Bible says: "Then were the days of unleavened bread." The passover (April 14th) had already come and gone." Ibid., 7.

6 "The next Passover was a year away!" Ibid., 7.

7 "But the pagan holiday of Easter was just a few days away. Remember! Herod was a pagan Roman who worshipped the "queen of heaven". He was NOT a Jew. He had no reason to keep the Jewish passover." Ibid., 7-8.

8 "It is elementary to see that Herod, in Acts 12, had arrested Peter during the days of unleavened bread, after the passover. The days of unleavened bread would end on the 21st of April. Shortly after that would come Herod's celebration of pagan Easter. Herod had not killed Peter during the days of unleavened bread simply because he wanted to wait until Easter. Since it is plain that both the Jews (Matt. 26:17- 47) and the Romans (Matt. 14:6-11) would kill during a religious celebration, Herod's opinion seemed that he was not going to let the Jews "have all the fun ". He would wait until his own pagan festival and see to it that Peter died in the excitement." (Gipp, 8)

Based upon this line of reasoning Gipp argues that God's providence led the King James translators to choose "Easter" in Acts 12:4 given the details of the context. "Easter" is not a mistranslation or an error in the KJB because "the Spirit-filled translators" knew that Luke was referring to the pagan festival in this context and rendered *pascha* accordingly.

> "Thus we see that it was God's providence which had the Spirit-filled translators of our Bible (King James) to CORRECTLY translate "pascha" as "Easter". It most certainly did not refer to the Jewish passover. In fact, to change it to "passover" would confuse the reader and make the truth of the situation unclear."[9]

The argument presented above by Dr. Gipp in defense of the KJB's use of "Easter" in Acts 12:4 is by no means unique to him. Similar arguments are found in a host of pro-King James literature. The following list is a mere sampling of volumes articulating similar arguments:

- Thomas Holland—*Crowned With Glory*, see pages 183-186.

- Floyd Nolan Jones—*Which Version is the Bible?*, see pages 76-77.

- D.A. Waite—*Defending the King James Bible*, see pages 240-241.

- D.A. Waite—*King James Bible Defined*, see page 1,451.

In summation, we see that the consensus defense given by King James apologists is built upon two assumptions: 1) the Jewish Passover

---

9 Ibid., 8.

had already passed; and 2) "Easter" is referring to a pagan celebration that Herod, a pagan king, would have been observing. Ironically on this point King James advocates agree with James R. White that "Easter" is pagan in origin, meaning, and application. White uses this view to justify his position that "Easter" is a mistranslation of the Greek word *pascha* whereas King James advocates defend the use of "Easter" because they believe that the context points to a pagan festival that Herod was observing.

For the sake of full disclosure, this author previously adhered to the common defense of "Easter" in Acts 12:4 presented by Dr. Gipp in *The Answer Book*. Prior to 2007, while still the Pastor of West Side Grace Church in Muskegon, MI, I taught Gipp's explanation in an Easter message to the believers in my assembly. In short, I accepted his teaching on the matter in an uncritical manner. More recent studies caused me to question the accuracy of Dr. Gipp's view.

Is "Easter" Exclusively Pagan?

An article posted to *KJV Today*'s website titled "'Easter' or 'Passover' in Acts 12:4?" first caused me to question the explanation provided by Dr. Gipp in the previous chapter. The article provides a framework for the discussion outlined in this chapter.[10] While the *KJV Today* article does a fair job of highlighting the etymological history of the English word "Easter;" it is ultimately incomplete. The article fails to discuss the historic connection in the English language between "Easter" and the Jewish feast commonly known as "Passover." Consequently, full agreement with the article's conclusion, that Easter in Acts 12:4 refers to a "Christian" holiday was not reached. Notwithstanding, the article is important in that it infuses an alternate narrative into the debate about "Easter" in Acts 12:4.

In order to satisfy the objections made by both King James advocates and critics we will consider the following in this chapter: 1) the influence of Alexander Hislop; 2) the etymology of "Easter"; 3) the Christian use of "Easter"; 4) the connection between "Easter" and Passover; and 4) other points to ponder.

---

10 "'Easter' or 'Passover' in Acts 12:4?" *King James Version Today*, www.kjvtoday.com/home/easter-or-passover-in-acts-124.

The Influence of Alexander Hislop

The true utility of the *KJV Today*'s article is found in that it serves to break the almost slavish connection between "Easter" and Ishtar/Astarte in the minds of many modern Christians on both sides of the textual debate. This connection can be traced back to the publication of *The Two Babylons* by Alexander Hislop in 1853. Hislop, an outspoken critic of Roman Catholicism falsely postulated an etymological relationship between "Easter" and Ishtar or Astarte based upon phonetic similarities. His argument is as follows:

> "What means the term Easter itself? It is not a Christian name. It bears its Chaldean origin on its very forehead. Easter is nothing else than Astarte, one of the titles of Beltis, the queen of heaven, whose name, as pronounced by the people of Nineveh, was evidently identical with that now in common use in this country. That name, as found by Layard on the Assyrian monuments, is Ishtar."[11]

The *KJV Today* article, on the contrary, argued that Ishtar/Astarte is not etymologically related to the word Easter.

> "While it is true that Ishtar (a form of Astarte) sounds similar to "Easter" the two words are not etymologically related. Astarte is "תורתשע (ashtarot)" in Hebrew. This name is derived from the word "הרתשע ('ashterâh)" which means "increase" or "flock" (Brown-Driver-Briggs' Hebrew Definitions). "הרתשע ('ashterâh)" is translated as "flocks" four times in the KJV. Hence, the name "Astarte" or "Ishtar" is a Semitic word related to animal fertility. This makes sense because Astarte was regarded as a goddess of fertility."

---

11 Hislop, Alexander. *The Two Babylons*. 1853,103.

Hislop's false etymological connection between "Easter" and Ishtar/Astarte was only one of his mistakes. As we will see in the next sub-point, the true origin of "Easter" is connected with the Anglo-Saxon goddess Eostre. More importantly, however, is his advancement of the fallacious notion that any word derived out of paganism mandates an absolute pagan meaning or connection in its later or even modern usage. For example, if one makes a dinner appointment for Thursday night are, they automatically worshipping the Norse god Thor; from whose name "Thursday" is derived? Of course not. They are just talking about what day of week they are going to meet someone for dinner. This highlights that the true error of Hislop is found in his confounding of a word's origin with its current usage. Just because a given English word is of pagan origin does not mandate pagan meaning in modern usage.

Brian Tegart, the author of another internet article titled, "Acts 12:4 – Passover and Easter" succinctly exposes Hislop's error.

> "...the idea that Easter is derived from Astarte/Ishtar seems to come first- or second-hand from Alexander Hislop's 1853 book *The Two Babylons*. As far as I can see, Hislop repeatedly makes the assertion of the connection between Easter and Astarte, but never provides any sources for his claim. What is entirely ironic is that Hislop is not arguing that "Easter" was associated with Astarte at the time of Herod - his argument is that "Easter" was originally entirely Christian but was corrupted by the Roman Catholic Church incorporating elements of pagan religions (including Astarte) in the 5th century A.D., long after Herod died. Despite this alleged connection of Astarte with Easter, many scholars now think

this connection is a "false etymology," meaning that it is only assumed correct because of the similar sounds between "Easter" and "Ishtar". Instead, the name "Easter" is probably derived from the Anglo-Saxon pagan goddess (post-dating Herod) of "Eostur" (and for those anti-Easter folk out there: even if the name has some pagan origins does not mean the Christian commemoration is therefore also pagan)."[12]

Once Hislop connected "Easter" and Isthar/Astarte it was picked up on by Fundamentalists and advanced in an uncritical and unverified manner. Consequently, the influence of Hislop looms large over the entire discussion of "Easter" in Acts 12:4, but it is an influence built upon incorrect reasoning, poor scholarship, and faulty assumptions.

The True Etymology of "Easter"

Accurately studying the etymology of "Easter," reveals that it has nothing to do with "flocks" or animal fertility. "Easter" ("Ostern" in German) is a Germanic word derived from the word "east" ("Ost" in German). The *Online Etymological Dictionary* is quoted in support:

> "Old English east "east, easterly, eastward," from Proto-Germanic *aus-to-, *austra- "east, toward the sunrise" (cf. Old Frisian ast "east," aster "eastward," Dutch oost Old Saxon ost, Old High German ostan, German Ost, Old Norse austr "from the east"), from PIE *aus- "to shine," especially "dawn" (cf. Sanskrit ushas "dawn;" Greek aurion "morning;" Old Irish usah, Lithuanian auszra "dawn;" Latin aurora "dawn," auster "south"), literally "to shine." The east is the direction in which dawn breaks."[13]

---

12 Brian Tegart. "Acts 12:4 – Passover and Easter" http://www.kjv-only.com/acts12_4.html.

13 "Easter" entry in the *Online Etymological Dictionary*. https://www.etymonline.com/

The *Oxford English Dictionary* (OED), the recognized authority on the history of the English language, is also in complete agreement with the *Online Etymological Dictionary* as to the etymology of the English word "Easter" (See Appendix A to read the OED's full etymological entry.):

> "Cognate with Old Dutch *ōster-* (in *ōstermānōth* April, lit. 'Easter-month'), Old Saxon *ōstar-* (in *ōstarfrisking* paschal lamb; Middle Low German *ōsteren* , *ōstern* , plural), Old High German *ōstara* (usually in plural *ōstarūn* ; Middle High German *ōster* (usually in plural *ōstern*), German *Ostern* , singular and (now chiefly regional) plural), probably < the same Germanic base as east *adv.* (and hence ultimately cognate with Sanskrit *uṣas* , Avestan *ušah-* , ancient Greek (Ionic and Epic) ἠώς , (Attic) ἕως , classical Latin *aurōra* , all in sense 'dawn'). For alternative (and less likely) etymologies see the references cited below. It is noteworthy that among the Germanic languages the word (as the name for Easter) is restricted to English and German; in other Germanic languages, as indeed in most European languages, the usual word for Easter is derived from the corresponding word for the Jewish Passover; compare pasch *n.* "

Simply stated, there is nothing in "East" that suggests animal fertility. Hence the word has nothing to do with Astarte or Ishtar. Relating the Germanic word "Easter" to the Semitic word "Ishtar" is as fallacious as relating the English word "Baby" to the Semitic word "Babylon," according to *KJV Today's* article.

Today, "east" refers to the direction from which the sun rises. The direction of "east" goes by that name because the Saxon word "east" meant "dawn", "sunrise" or "morning." Therefore, etymologically "Easter" basically means "dawn." According to the Venerable Bebe (672-735), the Old English word for the month of April was "Eosturmonað" or "East/Sunrise month." And "Eostre" came from the name of a Saxon spring fertility goddess who went by that name (Also see Appendix A).[14]

Christian Use of "Easter"

The fact that a Saxon goddess went by the name "Eostre" does not mean that "Easter" is a pagan word. Those who hold to this myth make it sound as if there was once a goddess with a certain name and Saxon Christians simply took that name arbitrarily without any biblical basis. If, for example, the pagans worshiped a goddess named "Sally" and Christians today refer to the day of the Lord's resurrection as "Sally", then surely, we have a problem. But that is not the case for Saxon Christians using "Easter" as the name of the day of the Lord's resurrection. As "easter" was a descriptive word that referred to the dawn or sunrise, we can understand why both pagans and Christians wished to use the word "east" for their respective purposes. Pagans wished to worship a goddess of sunrise, so they called her "Eostre". Christians on the other hand wished to celebrate a very special, but fundamentally different dawn, so they

---

14 See "Easter" or "Passover" in Acts 12:4?" at *KJV Today* website for a fuller discussion on the on the historical development of the word "Easter." http://www.kjvtoday.com/home/easter-or-passover-in-acts-124.

called the day "Easter." All four of the Gospel accounts in the New Testament describe Christ's resurrection as being discovered in the "morning" at "dawn" or at "the rising of the sun."

- Matthew 28:1—". . . as it began to **dawn** toward the first day of the week . . ."

- Mark 16:2—"And very early in the morning the first day of the week, they came unto the sepulchre **at the rising of the sun.**"

- Luke 24:1—"Now upon the first day of the week, **very early in the morning** . . ."

- John 20:1—"The first day of the week cometh Mary Magdalene early, **when it was yet dark. . .**"

One could view the resurrection morning as "dawn" *par excellence.* Per the OED, *par excellence* means "by virtue of special excellence or manifest superiority; pre-eminently; supremely, above all." There have been many dawns throughout history, but that special dawn on the day of Christ's resurrection is deserving of that noun more than any other. We often refer to notable biblical events using *par excellence* nouns, such as "the fall", "the flood", "the exodus", "the exile", "the advent,""the cross," etc. It should be expected then that ancient Saxon Christians might do the same with the resurrection in their own language. "Easter" therefore, is the Saxon word for this greatest dawn in all of history. By way of metonymical association, this term which refers to the "dawn" of the resurrection came to refer to the entire day of the resurrection.[15]

---

15   "'Easter' or 'Passover' in Acts 12:4?" *King James Version Today*, www.kjvtoday.com/

Furthermore, the imagery of "dawn" and the "rising of the sun" is not only reserved for the morning of Christ's bodily resurrection from the dead. The scriptures utilize the same imagery to describe the second Advent of the Lord Jesus Christ back to earth.

- Isaiah 60:1-3—"... to the brightness of thy rising."

- Malachi 4:2—"But unto you that fear my name shall the Sun of righteousness arise with healing in his wings;"

- Luke 1:76-79—"... whereby the dayspring from on high hath visited us ..."

- II Peter 1:19—"... until the day dawn, and the day star arise in your hearts:"

- Revelation 22:16—""I am the root and the offspring of David, and the bright and morning star."

Some Christians try to avoid anything that has to do with sunrise imagery, presuming that it is pagan. Yet, God in His Word compares Christ's second coming to the rising of the Sun. The word, "Easter," with its connotation to sunrise, pays tribute to this biblical imagery of Christ as the "Sun of righteousness".[16] The Old West-Saxon version of the Gospel of Luke translates the word as "eastdæle", which is the Saxon word for "east/sunrise". This is another proof that the word "Easter" came from the biblical language of the Saxons. Luke 1:78 in the West-Saxon translation of 990 reads as follows (note the bolded word **"eastdæle"**):

---

home/easter-or-passover-in-acts-124.

16 Malachi 4:2—But unto you that fear my name shall the Sun of righteousness arise with healing in his wings; and ye shall go forth, and grow up as calves of the stall.

- "Þurh innoþas ures godes mildheortnesse. on þam he us geneosode of **eastdæle** up springende;"

This connection between the eastern direction and the resurrection makes some Christians nervous about a possible pagan influence. However, there is no reason for such concern because this connection between the eastern direction and the verb "to rise" can be found in the New Testament itself.

> "The Greek verb "ανατελλω (anatello)" means "to rise" (*Thayer's Greek-English Lexicon*) and it is the word translated as "arise" in the above passage in II Peter 1:19 about Christ rising in our hearts [See verses above.]."[17]

The verb "ανατελλω" (to rise) is derived from the Greek word for "east," and the writers of the New Testament did not avoid using the verb despite this root. Still, any explanation that "Easter" is derived from a generic Saxon word for "dawn" that is not pagan in and of itself, does not seem to outweigh the mere possibility that a goddess went by the name of "Eostre" which scares some Christians into avoiding the word "Easter". These Christians need to realize that pagans should not be given monopoly over valid words in the English lexicon. We just must admit that the English language is the language of a people who were once pagan and that there are many vestiges of pagan etymology in English. Also, to be noted is the irony that the word "Ishtar," which some Christians wish to avoid, appears to be related

---

17   "'Easter' or 'Passover' in Acts 12:4?" *King James Version Today*, www.kjvtoday.com/home/easter-or-passover-in-acts-124.

to "Esther" which is the name of an entire book of the Holy Bible. Esther lived in a pagan culture and was given a pagan name as with Mordecai (which is related to the pagan god Marduk). While it has been demonstrated that "Easter" has nothing to do with Ishtar, the Bible itself shows that God can redeem a name even if it is in fact related to a pagan deity.[18]

The Connection Between "Easter" and Passover

According to the *Oxford English Dictionary*, "Easter" has a long history of being used as a reference to the Jewish "Passover," in addition to being used as a reference to the dawn/day of Christ's resurrection. The *KJV Today's* article completely overlooks this important and extremely relevant fact. The second definition provide for "Easter" in the OED reads as follows:

> "2. = Passover *n.* 1. Now only in **Jewish Easter** or with other contextual indication."

That is to say that the second definition of "Easter" is equivalent to the first definition of "Passover," according to the OED which is:

> "The major Jewish spring festival which commemorates the liberation of the People of Israel from Egyptian bondage, lasting seven days (in Israel) or eight days (in the Diaspora) from the 15th day of Nisan."

---

18 Ibid.

Additionally, the *Middle English Dictionary*, which supplies us with examples of the word "Easter's" usage in the 14th and 15th centuries confirms that "Easter" can be defined as "the Jewish Passover."[19]

Therefore, ample historical evidence exists from multiple English language resources that "Easter" was used to refer to the Jewish feast day before the word "Passover" was coined by Tyndale in 1530 in the early 16th century (See Appendix C).

Points to Ponder

While there is no doubt that many practices associated with the current cultural celebration known as "Easter" are pagan in origin; the word itself is not inextricably tied to paganism as many have claimed. For one to truly understand the motives of the King James translators in rendering the Greek word "*pascha*" as "Easter" in Acts 12:4, the connection between the English word "Easter" and paganism must be broken as an important first step.

Let the 1611 King James Bible stand as a case in point. If the King James translators understood "Easter" to be a reference to a pagan festival in Acts 12:4, why did they include a table in the front of the 1611 that would help the reader "To find Easter for ever" (See image below)?

---

19 https://quod.lib.umich.edu/m/middle-english-dictionary/dictionary/MED14534

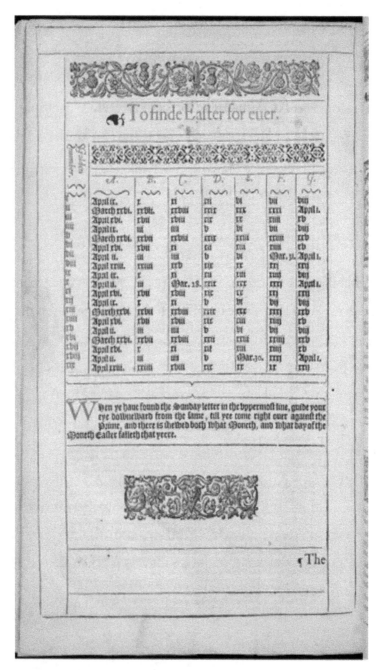

Working more than two hundred years before Hislop, the King James translators apparently knew something about the English word

"Easter" that Hislop did not know. If they thought "Easter" was exclusively pagan, they certainly would not have included such a table in the front of their translation to aid Christians in determining the timing of a pagan feast.

While the *KJV Today's* article is excellent in terms of highlining the etymological history of the English word "Easter;" this author does not agree with their overall conclusion about the meaning of "Easter" in Acts 12:4. Luke is not referring to the Christian festival of "Easter" but to Jewish feast day of "Passover" as we will demonstrate in the next chapter. Not only does the English word "Easter" refer to the morning of the resurrection, but it was also used interchangeably with the word "Passover" to refer to the Jewish festival. As we conclude this Chapter, here are a couple of points for the reader to consider:

- Frist, why did Dr. Samuel C. Gipp, an outspoken proponent of the 1611 edition of the King James Bible, not consider the table found within it for calculating the date of "Easter" into his explanation of the word's meaning?

- Second, recall from the Introduction that Dr. James R. White also embraced the notion that "Easter" was an exclusively pagan word and therefore not an appropriate translation of *pascha* in Acts 12:4. Why does White, an opponent of Gipp's, not refute the King James Only understanding of the word "Easter" based upon a more accurate etymological history of the word?

As it turns out, scholars on both sides of the textual debate have not been very scholarly.

"Easter" in the English Bible: A Brief Look at the History of Translation

This chapter, will seek to demonstrate the following: 1) "Easter" was used for centuries as a reference to the Jewish feast before Tyndale coined the term "Passover" in 1530; 2) the Greek word *pascha* was translated as "Easter" in English as a reference to the Jewish holy day both before and after 1530. Therefore, the notion that *pascha* NEVER meant "Easter" in English is an error contrary to history.

John Wycliffe translated the Bible from Latin into Middle English in the late 14th century. In his groundbreaking work he decided to transliterate the Latin equivalent of *pascha* into Middle English as "pask" or "paske" all 29 times it is used in the New Testament. Translators of the English Bible during the early Reformation of the 1500s adopted a similar practice but on a more limited scope. For example, Tyndale (1526), Coverdale (1535), and Matthews (1537) each rendered *pascha* as some form of "pascall" at least once in their respective translations.

- Tyndale (1526)—used a form of "paschal" three different times:

    ◦ "paschal" (Matthew 26:17)

    ◦ "pascall lambe" (Mark 14:12 & John 18:28)

- Coverdale (1535)—used a form of "paschal" one time:

    ◦ "pascall lambe" in John 18:28

- Matthews (1537)—followed Tyndale in using a form of "paschal" three different times:

    ◦ "paschal" (Matthew 26:17)

    ◦ "pascall lambe" (Mark 14:12 & John 18:28)

William Tyndale (1526)

Being the pioneer of these early translators, it is imperative that we study Tyndale's work on this matter in detail. Above we noted the three times Tyndale rendered *pascha* as some form of "paschal." But what about the other 26 occurrences of *pascha* in the *Textus Receptus*? Without exception, in every one of these 26 occurrences Tyndale translated *pascha* as some form of "Easter" (See the table in Appendix D for a complete catalogue of occurrences.). The "Easter" occurrences are as follows:

- "ester"—15 times

- "esterlambe"—3 times

- "ester lambe"—7 times

- "feeste of ester"—1 time.

So, we see that Tyndale associated the word "Easter" with the Greek *pascha* 26 times. Translating from exile in Germany in 1526, Tyndale was influenced by Martin Luther's earlier German translation of the *Textus Receptus* from 1522. As you may recall from the previous chapter the etymology of the English word "Easter," is impacted by the Old Germanic word "Oster." Every time, without exception, that the Greek word *pascha* occurred in the New Testament text, Luther rendered it as some form of "Oster" in German which equals "Easter" in English. Luther's "Oester" usages are as follows (Also see Appendix D):

- "Ostern"—16 times
- "Osterlamm"—12 times
- "Osterfest"—1 time.

Before going any further we need to acknowledge two important conclusions: 1) Luther and Tyndale clearly *did not* think that "Easter" was pagan or they would not have used that word when translating into their respective languages, and 2) the notion that *pascha* **never** meant "Easter" in English has been proven false.

In the previous chapter it was stated that according to the *Middle English Dictionary*, "Easter" was being used in the 14th and 15th centuries to refer to "The Jewish Passover" over two hundred years before Tyndale invented the term "Passover" in 1530. The WestSaxon Gospels from 990 and 1175 use some form of "Easter" exclusively in their respective texts to refer to "The Jewish Passover," just as the *Middle English Dictionary* asserted (see Appendix B). The WestSaxon

Gospels clinch the argument that "Easter" was not an exclusively pagan word as well as prove beyond doubt that "Easter" was used for centuries to refer to the Jewish "Passover" in the Biblical text. In short, *pascha* meant "Easter" in English before the word "Passover" was even coined by Tyndale in 1530 when he was working on his translation of the Pentateuch. The *Oxford English Dictionary* confirms this by reporting that the first known usage of the word "Passover" in English can be found in Tyndale's translation of the Pentateuch from 1530, in which he translates the Hebrew word "*pecah*" as "Passover" all 22 times the word is used in Genesis through Deuteronomy (See OED entry for "Passover" in Appendix C).

Miles Coverdale (1535)

In 1535, Miles Coverdale published the first complete translation of the Bible into English. Coverdale had access to Tyndale's work to inform his translation of the New Testament as well as the Pentateuch. This does not mean however, that Coverdale followed Tyndale with exact identicality.

Above we saw that all 22 times that the Hebrew word *pecach* occurred in the Pentateuch, Tyndale rendered it as "Passover" in English. Of these 22 occurrences in the Pentateuch, Coverdale translated *pecach* as "Passover" five times and some form of "Easter" 17 times.

- "Passover"—Exodus 12:11, 21, 27, 43, 48

- "Easterfeast"—Exodus 34:25

- "Lord's Easter"—Leviticus 23:5

- "Easter"—Numbers 9:2, 4-6, 10, 12-14 (2x), 16, 28:16, 33:3; Deuteronomy 16:1, 2, 5-6

All told, of the 48 occurrences of the word "Passover" in the Old Testament, 25 times Coverdale used the English word "Easter." The remaining 23 times he used the English word "Passover." Therefore, it is clear that Coverdale viewed "Easter" and "Passover" as interchangeable terms to describe the Jewish feast. In fact, in his translation of II Chronicles 30, Coverdale uses these terms interchangeably in the same context!

- II Chronicles 30:1-2—And Hezekiah sent into all Israel and Judah, and wrote letters unto Ephraim and Manasseh, that they should come to the house of the LORDE at Jerusalem, to keep **easter** unto the LORDE God of Israel. And the king held a council with his rulers, and all the congregation at Jerusalem, to keep **Passover** in the second month:

- II Chronicles 30:5—And they appointed it to be proclaimed throughout all Israel from Beer-sheba unto Dan, that they should come to keep **Passover** unto the LORDE God of Israel: for they were not many to keep it as it is written.

- II Chronicles 30:15—and slew the **Passover** on the fourteenth day of the second month. And ye priests and Levites were ashamed, and hallowed themselves, and brought the burnt offerings to the house of the LORDE,

- II Chronicles 30:18—There were many people also of Ephraim, Manasseh, Issachar and Zebulon, which were not clean, but ate the **Easter** lamb not as it is written: for Hezekiah prayed for them, and said: The LORDE, which is gracious,

In terms of the New Testament, Coverdale expanded the connection between the Greek word *pascha* and the English word "Easter" in his 1535 New Testament. In 1526 Tyndale used the word "Easter" 26 times whereas Coverdale used it 28 times in 1535. Even after the word "Passover" was coined by Tyndale in 1530, His contemporaries did not immediately replace "Easter" as the preferred translation of *pascha* (See Appendix D).

Matthew's Bible (1537)

The Matthew's Bible was published in 1537 by John Rodgers under the pseudonym Thomas Matthews, during a time when printing the Bible in English was both illegal and risky. Rodgers' translation was largely identical to that of Coverdale's in at least half the work, according to English Bible historian David Norton.[20]

The Matthew's Bible nearly standardized the use of the English word "Passover" in the Old Testament by utilizing it 47 out of 48 times (Ezekiel 45:21 contains the sole occurrence of "Easter" in Matthew's Old Testament). The same, however, could not be said for the New Testament. Rodgers followed Tyndale in translating the Greek word *pascha* as some form of "paschal" three times and some form of "Easter" 26 times. The verses in which these various forms

---

20 Norton, David. *The King James Bible: A Short History from Tyndale to Today.* Cambridge University Press, 2011.

are used are identical between the work of Tyndale and Rodgers (See Appendix D). From this we see once again that "Passover" had not yet supplanted "Easter" as the preferred English translation of *pascha*.

Great Bible (1539)

The next English translation, also conducted by Miles Coverdale, was the Great Bible of 1539, or the Cranmer's Bible because of the preface by the Archbishop included in the second edition onwards. "It was the first major revision [of Tyndale] done under the auspices of the English Church."[21]

In terms of the Old Testament, the Great Bible was similar to the Matthews Bible in that it used the word "Passover" 47 out of 48 times. However, The Great Bible, like the Matthews Bible, utilized "Easter" in Ezekiel 45:21:

- Matthews Bible—Upon the xiiij. day of the first month ye shall keep **Easter**. Seven days shall the feast continue wherein there shall no sower nor leavened bred be eaten.

- Great Bible—Upon the .xiiij. day of the first month, ye shall keep **easter**. Seven days shall the feast continue, where there shall no swore nor leavened breed be eaten.

The same, however, cannot be said for the Great Bible's New Testament text. Of all the Reformation Era, English Bibles we have looked at so far, the Great Bible exhibits the most diversity in terms of how the Greek word *pascha* was translated in the New Testament.

---

21 Ibid., 17

In fact, there is almost an even split between the use of "Easter" and "Passover" in the Great Bible's New Testament. Of the 29 times that *pascha* occurs in the text, the Great Bible uses a form of "Easter" 15 times and "Passover" 14 times. The Great Bible even uses these English words interchangeably within the same context in multiple different passages. Please consider the following examples from Matthew 26, Luke 22, and John 18.

- Mathew 26

    ○ Matthew 26:2—ye know that after two days shall be **Easter**, and the son of man shall be delivered over, to be crucified.

    ○ Matthew 26:17—The first day of sweet breed, the disciples came to Jesus, saying unto him: where wilt thou that we prepare for the, to eat the **Passover?**

    ○ Matthew 26:18—And he said: go into the city, to such a man, and say unto him, the master sayeth: my time is at hand, I will keep mine **Easter** by the, with my disciples:

    ○ Matthew 26:19—And the disciples did as Jesus had appointed them, and they made ready the **Passover**.

- Luke 22

    ○ Luke 22:1—"The feast of sweet breed drew nigh, which is called **Easter**,"

- Luke 22:7-8— Then came the day of sweet breed, when of necessity **Passover** must be offered. And he sent Peter & John, saying: go & prepare us the Passover, that we may eat.

  - See also Luke 22:11, 13, 15— where the word "**Passover**" is used.

- John 18

  - John 18:28—Then led they Jesus from Caiaphas into the hall of judgment. It was in the morning, & they them selves went not into the judgment hall lest they should be defiled, but that they might eat **Passover**.

  - John 18:39—Ye have a custom, that I should deliver you one loose at **Easter**. Will ye that I lose unto you the king of the Jews?

Translated in 1539, nine years after Tyndale coined the term "Passover" in 1530, the Great Bible is the first English New Testament to connect the Greek word *pascha* with the newly minted English word "Passover." The move to use "Passover" nearly half of the time in the Great Bible is representative of a growing expectance and confidence in the word "Passover's" ability to communicate the sense of the Greek text in English. Notice, however, that it took thirteen years (1526-1539) for the Greek word *pascha* to be connected with the English word "Passover." Even after the word "Passover" was coined, it took nine years (1530-1539) and three English translations for the connection between *pascha* and "Passover" to be formally established. Consequently, the notion that *pascha* never meant "Easter" in English is adequately proven false. The connection had been established and in use for thirteen years in three different English translations before "Passover" first appeared in the New Testament text of an English Bible.

Geneva New Testament (1557)

After the publication of the Great Bible in 1539 the English-speaking world would have to wait eighteen years before a new transition of the Bible would appear. This new translation was the 1557 Geneva New Testament. According to English Bible historian David Norton, "The Geneva Bible was the first truly collaborative English version. It was the work of a dozen or so Protestant scholars living in exile from an England that had returned to Catholicism under Queen Mary. The leader was William Whittingham who had produced a remarkable preliminary draft [of the KJB], the 1557 Geneva NT."[22] Three years later, in 1560, a complete Bible would be published by these Genevan exiles.

Rather than follow the Great Bible in expanding the use of "Passover" in the New Testament, the 1557 Geneva New Testament significantly reversed the trend. The English word "Passover" is only found *three* times in the 1557 Geneva New Testament (Matthew 26:17, 19; Luke 22:7). Twice the term "Pascal lambe" is used (Mark 14:12; John 18:28) by the Genevan exiles, a phrase that did *not* appear in the Great Bible. The remaining 24 occurrences of *pascha*

---

22 Ibid., 19

were rendered as some form of "Easter" in the 1557 Geneva New Testament. One similarity between the Great Bible and Geneva New Testament of 1557 was that "Passover" and "Easter" were used interchangeably in Matthew 26 (See the example for Matthew 26 above.).

Geneva Bible (1560)

When the Geneva Bible was published complete with Old and New Testaments in 1560 it was the first English translation to use the word "Passover" all 29 times that *pascha* is found in the *Textus Receptus*. By 1560, 34 years of historical precedent had been established in terms of using the English word "Easter" to express the Greek word *pascha*. In addition, 21 years of translational tradition existed from 1539 to 1560 during which the English words "Easter" and "Passover" were used as synonymous terms. In terms of the history of the English Bible, the Geneva's exclusive use of "Passover" to convey the truth of *pascha* in English was the exception rather than the rule.

Bishops Bible (1568)

The Bishops Bible of 1568 was the second official Bible of the English Church. It was intended to be a revision of and replacement for the Great Bible from 1539 in terms of official use in the Anglican Church. As its title suggests, it was primarily the work of Anglican Bishops.[23] (Norton, 22-25)

Even though the 1560 Geneva Bible adopted the exclusive use of "Passover" in the New Testament the Bishops Bible did not follow

---

23 Ibid., 22-15.

suit. The Bishops Bible retained the use of Easter on three occasions in two verses:

- John 11:55—And the **Jewes Easter** was nigh at hand, and many went out of the country up to Jerusalem before the **Easter,** to purify them selves.

- Acts 12:4—And when he had caught him, he put him in prison also, and delivered him to four quaternions of soldiers to be kept, intending after **Easter** to bring him forth to the people.

It is clear from an examination of the context of John 11:55 that what the Bishops Bible calls the "Jews Easter" is everywhere else in the gospels referred to as "Passover." Furthermore, three verses later in John 12:1 the Bishops Bible mentions "Passouer." Therefore, there is no doubt that the two English words were viewed as a reference to the same event.

- John 12:1—"Then Jesus, six days before the **Passover,** came to Bethanie, where Lazarus had ben dead, whom he raised from death."

The rendering of "Easter" in Acts 12:4 in the Bishops Bible is of critical importance. First, there is no reason within the Bishops Bible to think that "Easter" in Acts 12:4 is referring to something different from the "Jews Easter" in John 11:55 i.e., the "Passover?" Second, the translators of the King James Bible were given a rule[24] by

---

24 Rule 1: The ordinary Bible read in the Church, commonly called the Bishops' Bible, to be followed, and as little altered as the truth of the original will permit.

Bishop Bancroft that the Bishops Bible was to serve as the base text for their translation. When the King James translators left the word "Easter" in Acts 12:4 they were following this directive. The Bishops Bible had "Easter" in Act 12:4 and the King James translations saw no reason to alter the text. This chronologically brings us to the Bible at issue, the 1611 King James Bible.

King James (1611)

By the time we get to the publication of the KJB in 1611 there is roughly 80 years of translational precedent regarding the interchangeable use of "Easter" and "Passover" in the English Bible, even after the term "Passover" was coined by Tyndale in 1530. In the early 17th century, both words were perfectly acceptable ways of capturing the sense of the Greek word *pascha* in English. The sole use of the word "Easter" in the King James Bible is as follows:

- Acts 12:4—"And when he had apprehended him, he put him in prison, and delivered him to four quaternions of soldiers to keep him, intending after **Easter** to bring him forth to the people."

Because Acts 12:4 is the only occurrence of "Easter" in that KJB that means the translators opted to alter the Bishop's Bible in John 11:5 (See pervious section for the Bishops reading of this verse.). The Oxford Company, which translated the four Gospels and the Book of Acts for the KJB is responsible for these decisions. Twice they elected to change the rendering of *pascha* from "Easter" to "Passover" in John 11:5 and once they decided to leave it as "Easter" in Acts 12:4.

When the translators made this decision, were they intending to refer to a pagan festival celebrated by Herod in Acts 12:4 or were they simply using an acceptable English synonym for Jewish "Passover?" Given the totality of the evidence presented in this chapter, it makes far more sense to view "Easter" in Acts 12:4 as a reference to the Jewish festival of "Passover" than it does to think that the King James translators ascribed a meaning to the word "Easter" wholly apart from the way that that word was used and understood by their predecessors and contemporaries. In short, when they used "Easter" in Acts 12:4 they were referring to "Passover" *not* a pagan festival celebrated by Herod or a Christian holiday as asserted by the *KJV Today* article cited in the previous chapter.

Once again, we turn to the *Oxford English Dictionary*. Earlier we established that, according to the OED, "Easter" and "Passover" mean the same thing. Clinching the point are the historical word usage examples provided in the OED's entry for "Easter", two of which are scriptural in nature:

> "1535 Bible (Coverdale) Ezekiel xlv. 21 Upon ye xiiij. day of the first month ye shall keep **Easter**.
>
> 1611 Bible (King James) Acts xii. 4 Intending after **Easter** to bring him forth."[25]

The OED cites Acts 12:4 in the KJB as an example of "Easter" being used as a refernce to the Jewish "Passover."

The most authoritative source on the history of the English language just said that "Easter" in Acts 12:4 is a reference to "Passover."

---

25 See Appendix B to view a photo of the OED's entry for "Easter."

When the King James translators rendered *pascah* as "Easter" in Acts 12:4 they were referring to the Jewish "Passover" not a pagan holiday or a Christian festival.

Thus far, we have debunked the following myths: 1) "Easter" is an exclusively pagan word; 2) the Greek word *pascha* NEVER meant "Easter" in English; 3) the English word "Easter" has no association to the Jewish feast day of "Passover." Additionally, we have proved beyond historical doubt that *pascha* meant "Easter" in English before the word "Passover" even existed. Likewise, we have demonstrated that, even after the invention of the word "Passover" by Tyndale in 1530, the two words were used interchangeably to refer to the Jewish feast.

So then why did neither Samuel C. Gipp nor James R. White (along with various other scholars) discuss any of these FACTS in their respective discussions of "Easter" in Acts 12:4?

All that remains is to demonstrate that "Passover" is an acceptable Biblical term to refer to the entire paschal week i.e., Passover (14th) and Days Unleavened Bread (15th-21st). In the next chapter, we will seek to demonstrate this connection and check out the scriptural veracity for the conclusion that "Easter" in Acts 12:4 in the King James Bible is a reference to the Jewish "Passover."

Scriptural Exposition of Acts 12:4

Having proved our case regarding the etymology and translational history of the English word "Easter" almost to the point of *ad nauseum*, we will now demonstrate that Luke, the author of Acts, is referring to the Jewish feast day in Acts 12:1–4:

> Now about that time Herod the king stretched forth his hands to vex certain of the church.
>
> And he killed James the brother of John with the sword.
>
> And because he saw it pleased the Jews, he proceeded further to take Peter also. (Then were the days of unleavened bread.)
>
> And when he had apprehended him, he put him in prison, and delivered him to four quaternions of soldiers to keep him; intending after Easter to bring him forth to the people. (Acts 12:1–4)

In the context of Acts 12:1, Herod is NOT seeking to "vex" the church the body of Christ; but rather the Jewish Kingdom Church at Jerusalem. Herod's vexation of the church in verse 1 takes the form of the execution of "James the brother of John" in verse 2. James was one stles chosen by Christ during his earthly ministry.[26]

that the murder of James pleased the Jewish people,

...gious leadership of Israel, he decided to arrest Peter

as well (Acts 12:3). The same Jewish leadership Herod was seeking

to please had long sought to punish the Jerusalem congregation and

its leaders i.e., the 12 Apostles.[27] Therefore, they are very pleased with

Herod's actions against Peter.

---

26 This point is demonstrated in the following passages:

Matthew 4:21-22—And going on from thence, he saw other two brethren, James the son of Zebedee, and John his brother, in a ship with Zebedee their father, mending their nets; and he called them. 22) And they immediately left the ship and their father, and followed him.

Matthew 10:2—Now the names of the twelve apostles are these; The first, Simon, who is called Peter, and Andrew his brother; James the son of Zebedee, and John his brother;

Matthew 19:28— And Jesus said unto them, Verily I say unto you, That ye which have followed me, in the regeneration when the Son of man shall sit in the throne of his glory, ye also shall sit upon twelve thrones, judging the twelve tribes of Israel.

27 This point is demonstrated in the following passages:

Acts 4:17-21—But that it spread no further among the people, let us straitly threaten them, that they speak henceforth to no man in this name. 18) And they called them, and commanded them not to speak at all nor teach in the name of Jesus. 19) But Peter and John answered and said unto them, Whether it be right in the sight of God to hearken unto you more than unto God, judge ye. 20) For we cannot but speak the things which we have seen and heard. 21) So when they had further threatened them, they let them go, finding nothing how they might punish them, because of the people: for all men glorified God for that which was done.

Acts 5:17-19—Then the high priest rose up, and all they that were with him, (which is the sect of the Sadducees,) and were filled with indignation, 18) And laid their hands on the apostles, and put them in the common prison.19) But the angel of the Lord by night opened the prison doors, and brought them forth, and said,

Acts 5:40—And to him they agreed: and when they had called the apostles, and beaten them, they commanded that they should not speak in the name of Jesus, and let them go.

Acts 8:1—And Saul was consenting unto his death. And at that time there was a great persecution against the church which was at Jerusalem; and they were all scattered abroad throughout the regions of Judaea and Samaria, except the apostles.

Acts 9:1-2— And Saul, yet breathing out threatenings and slaughter against the disciples of the Lord, went unto the high priest, 2) And desired of him letters to Damascus to the synagogues, that if he found any of this way, whether they were men or women, he might bring them bound unto Jerusalem.

Luke makes the timing of Peter's apprehension clear with the parenthetical statement in Acts 12:3, "then were the days of unleavened bread." Herod arrested Peter and placed him under guard, "intending after Easter to bring him forth to the people." We gather from the context that "the people" in verse 4 are "the Jews" in verse 3, the very same group that was pleased with Herod's arrest of Peter.

Mark well that these verses say nothing about Herod keeping or observing anything, much less the pagan spring festival of "Easter" as defined by Hislop. The people observing something in the context are the Jews whom Herod was aiming to please by arresting Peter. What were the Jews observing at the time? "The days of unleavened bread" as verse 3 clearly states. The most natural reading of these verses is that Herod elected to hold Peter until after the conclusion of the feast that the Jews were observing, not a pagan festival, which neither a modern nor ancient reader would discern from the text.

As we have already proven, "Easter" is a synonym for "Passover." Therefore, the most natural reading of Acts 12:3-4 is that Herod would bring Peter forth unto the people after the conclusion of Jewish feast of "Easter/Passover."

Recall the arguments presented by Dr. Samuel C. Gipp in *The Answer Book* presented in Chapter One. He concluded that Luke could not have been referring to the Jewish "Passover" in Acts 12:4 for the following reasons:

- "Easter" is an ancient pagan holiday connected with the worship of the goddesses Astarte and Ishtar.

- Passover occurred on the 14th of the month—no event after the 14th is EVER referred to as Passover (Exodus 12:13-18; Numbers 28:16-18; Deuteronomy 16:1-8).

- The Days of Unleavened Bread began on the 15th of the month, the day after Passover. The Days of Unleavened Bread are ALWAYS after Passover and are NEVER referred to as Passover.

- Peter was arrested during the Days of Unleavened Bread which are AFTER Passover.

- Therefore, Herod could not possibly have been referring to Passover in Acts 12:4. The next Passover was a year away.

- Herod was a pagan Roman who worshiped the queen of heaven and had no reason to keep the Jewish Passover.

- Herod did not kill Peter during the Days of Unleavened Bread because he wanted to wait until later in the month after the Passing of his own holiday i.e., Easter.

So, per Dr. Gipp, Luke could not have been referring to the Jewish "Passover" in Acts 12:4 because Peter was arrested during the "days of unleavened bread" which were after "Passover" from the 15th till the 21st of the month. According to Dr. Gipp, no day after the 14th is EVER referred to as "Passover" in scripture.

It's interesting then, that Dr. Gipp does not bring Ezekiel 45:21, Matthew 26:17-18, or Luke 22:1 into the discussion. These verses connect or include the "days of unleavened bread" with the "Passover:"

- Ezekiel 45:21—"In the first month, in the fourteenth day of the month, ye shall have the **passover, a feast of seven days; unleavened bread shall be eaten.**"

- Matthew 26:17-18—"Now **the first day of the feast of unleavened bread** the disciples came to Jesus, saying unto him, **Where wilt thou that we prepare for thee to eat the passover?** And he said, Go into the city to such a man, and say unto him, The Master saith, My time is at hand; **I will keep the passover** at thy house with my disciples."

- Luke 22:1—"Now **the feast of unleavened bread drew nigh, which is called the Passover.**"

The Ezekiel passage clearly states that "passover" was a feast of seven days that began on the 14th of the month during which unleavened bread was eaten. In Matthew the Apostles approached Jesus about eating the "Passover" on the first day of the "feast of unleavened bread." If Gipp's exposition in *The Answer Book* is correct, the Apostles would have be acting contrary to Old Testament practice! Adding insult to injury, Jesus does not rebuke or correct the Apostles' false practice but agrees to eat the "Passover" with his disciples on "the first day of the feast of unleavened bread". According to Gipp's explanation, Christ would be violating the Old Testament scriptures; a claim no honest theologian intends to make regarding the Lord Jesus Christ. Perhaps most condemning to Gipp's position, is Luke, the same person who wrote Acts 12:4 explicitly states in Luke 22:1 that the "feast of unleavened bread" was called "Passover." It would therefore be expected for him to continue this usage in later writings.

These verses explain why Luke included the parenthetical statement about the "days of unleavened bread" at the end of Acts 12:3. He did so to help the reader identify the timing of Peter's arrest by Herod. As the second part of a two part "treatise" addressed to Theophilus (see Luke 1:1-4 & Acts 1:1), the connection between Luke 22:1 and Acts 12:3-4 would have been clear to Theophilus. Luke is clearly reporting that Peter was arrested by Herod during the Jewish paschal or "Passover" week as identified by Ezekiel 45:21, Matthew 26:17-18, and Luke 22:1. Because he sought to please the Jews in Acts 12:3, Herod elected to hold Peter until after "Passover" or "Easter" (when properly defined) before bringing "him forth to the people."

In summary the context of Acts 12 is thoroughly Jewish, not pagan, and the English word "Easter" has a long history of being used as a reference to the Jewish feast, that predates the use of the phrase "Passover". The King James translators used "Easter" in Acts 12:4 to refer to the Jewish festival and not a pagan festival. This is the simplest, most Biblical, and most charitable answer to the alleged controversy. The King James Bible is, therefore, not in error with this rendering nor is it a mistranslation of the Greek word *pascha*. Rather it is a perfectly acceptable English way of referring to the Jewish feast, as attested by the etymological and translational evidence already discussed.

The uniformity in phrasing we see in modern translations was not a burden that the King James translators placed upon themselves. According to the Preface to the 1611, The King James translators did not employ a principle of rigidity when taking words from the donor language (Hebrew/Greek) and rendering them in the receptor language (English).

> "Another thing we think good to admonish thee of, gentle reader that we have not tied ourselves to an **uniformity of phrasing**, or to an identity of words, as some peradventure would wish that we had done, because they observe, that some learned men somewhere, have been as exact as they could that way. Truly, that we might not vary from the sense of that which we had translated before, if the word signified that same in both places (for there be some words that be not the same sense everywhere) we were especially careful, and made a conscience, according to our duty. But, that we should express the same notion in the same particular word; as for example, if we translate the Hebrew or Greek word once by PURPOSE, never to call it INTENT; if one where JOURNEYING, never TRAVELING; if one where THINK, never SUPPOSE; if one where PAIN, never ACHE; if one where JOY, never GLADNESS, etc. Thus to mince the matter, we thought to savour more of curiosity than wisdom, and that rather it would breed scorn in the Atheist, than bring profit to the godly Reader. For is the kingdom of God to become words or syllables? Why should we be in bondage to them if we may be free, use one precisely when we may use another no less fit, as commodiously?"

This means that in the minds of the King James translators there are multiple acceptable ways of saying the same thing. The decision to employ diversity of phrasing was made on purpose by the translators, so as to enrich the translation despite their knowledge that some would take issue with the practice. As long as an English word fit the sense of the Hebrew or Greek in a given passage; the King James translators did not lock themselves into rendering a given word from the donor language with the same word in the receptor language every time. Such is the case with how the translators chose to handle the Greek word *pascha*; either "Easter" or "Passover" were well suited for conveying the idea of the Jewish feast in English.

How Did Gipp Get it So Wrong?

We have now shown that the King James Bible is correct in Acts 12:4 but not for the reasons identified by Dr. Gipp or those espoused by any other King James advocate yet encountered. Most King James Only advocates offer some form of the Gipp argument presented in *The Answer Book* for why "Easter" is correct in Acts 12:4. Essentially, Dr. Gipp and those who argue similarly make mistakes in each of the following three categories: definitional, scriptural, and theological/dispensational.

Definitional

The definitional mistake here is found in substituting Hislop's false etymology regarding Ishtar/Astarte for the true etymology set forth in the *Oxford English Dictionary*, *Online Etymology Dictionary*, and the *Middle English Dictionary*. Moreover, Dr. Gipp makes no attempt to discuss the pre-1611 translational history of the word "Easter" in the English Bible.

Scriptural

Dr. Gipp fails to compare scripture with scripture when he tells his readers that no other day other than the 14th of Nisan is EVER referred to as "Passover." This is completely false as demonstrated by Ezekiel 45:21 and Luke 22:1; verses that Dr. Gipp conveniently left out of his explanation. Why would Dr. Gipp leave these verses out his explanation?

The answer is because he must! In this way, we see the tension between the scriptures and false etymology created by Hislop and embraced by Dr. Gipp. In an effort to explain why the KJB is not mistaken in its use of "Easter" in Acts 12:4, as Dr. Gipp has defined the term, he must overlook Ezekiel 45:21 and Luke 22:1 because they do not fit the paradigm he is seeking to advance. If "Passover" is used to refer to anything beyond the 14th even once, or could be proven to include the "days of unleavened bread" which began on the 15th and ended on the 21st, then the modern versions would be right and the King James would be wrong, according to the way Gipp has structured his argument:

> "Problem: Even though the Jewish passover was held in mid-April (the fourteenth) and the pagan festival Easter was held later the same month, how do we know that Herod was referring to Easter in Acts 12:4 and not the Jewish passover? If he was referring to the passover, the translation of "pascha" as "Easter" is incorrect. **If he was indeed referring to the pagan holyday (holiday) Easter, then the King James Bible (1611) must truly be the very word and words of God for it is the only Bible in print today which has the correct reading.**"[28]

---

28 Gipp, Samuel C. *The Answer Book: A Help Book for Christians.* Bible & Literature Missionary Foundation: Shelbyville, TN: 1989., 4

Before moving off this point, a further observation regarding Dr. Gipp's argument is in order. Above we noted that Dr. Gipp failed to acknowledge the connection between "Passover" and the "days of unleavened bread" in Matthew 26:17-18. This oversight on Gipp's part is curious given the fact that he clearly references Matthew 26:17-19 on *TWO* different occasions in his defense for why "Easter" is not a mistake in the KJB. Twice on the same page Dr. Gipp uses Matthew 26:17-18 to support an alternative point about the Jews not being averse to killing Christ during the feast of "Passover."

> "Second, he could not have been waiting until after the passover because he thought the Jews would not kill a man during a religious holiday. They had killed Jesus during passover (**Matthew 26:17-19**,47). They were also excited about Herod's murder of James. Anyone knows that a mob possesses the courage to do violent acts during religious festivities, not after. . . It is elementary to see that Herod, in Acts 12, had arrested Peter during the days of unleavened bread, **after the passover**. The days of unleavened bread would end on the 21st of April. Shortly after that would come Herod's celebration of pagan Easter. Herod had not killed Peter during the days of unleavened bread simply because he wanted to wait until **Easter**. Since it is plain that both the Jews (**Matthew 26:17- 47**) and the Romans (Matthew 14:6-11) would kill during a religious celebration, Herod's opinion seemed that he was not going to let the Jews "have all the fun ". He would wait until his own pagan festival and see to it that Peter died in the excitement."[29]

---

29 Ibid., 8

From this we observe that Gipp referenced a passage (Matt. 26:17-18) that contradicts the point he is endeavoring to make in the very paragraph in which he referenced it. We might then conclude that Dr. Gipp knows how to use a concordance and was very aware of verses such as Ezekiel 45:21, Matthew 26:17-18, and Luke 22:1; but chose to ignore them in his exposition because they did not fit the doctrinal paradigm he was seeking to advance. A dangerous practice indeed for any theologian or apologist.

Theological/Dispensational

Dr. Gipp's exposition is theologically and dispensationally confused. At one point, he offers the following reason why Herod would not have waited until after "Passover" to release Peter:

> "...Peter was no longer considered a Jew. He had repudiated Judaism. The Jews would have no reason to be upset by Herod's actions."[30]

Is this an accurate statement? Had Peter, the leader of the Little Flock "repudiated Judaism?" Did we not observe above that Peter and the other Apostles were laboring during the early Acts period to save their kinsman according to the flesh? It was Peter and the Apostles who stayed in Jerusalem when the persecution broke out following the death of Stephen (Acts 8:1). The bottom line here is this; Gipp's assessment of what is going on in Acts 12 is based at least in part on a faulty dispensational theology. Peter agrees to limit his ministry at

---

30 Ibid., 8

the Jerusalem Council in Acts 15 to the circumcision (Gal. 2:9), after Gipp says that Peter has "repudiated Judaism" as of Acts 12.

Furthermore, in the context of Acts 12, the Jews had not asked Herod to do anything with respect to Peter. Herod's actions were his own when he saw how happy the Jewish leadership was on account of his actions toward James in verse one. The circumstances were completely different in Acts 12 than they were in Matthew 26 when the Jews demanded the execution of Jesus. Rather than create a scene by executing Peter during the Jewish feast of Passover/Unleavened Bread, Herod elected to wait until after the paschal week was over.

We now sufficiently see that a matrix of poor definitional, scriptural, and theological/dispensational thinking caused Dr. Gipp to misidentify the events of Acts 12.

The Christian "Passover" View

More informed defenders of the KJB have advanced a different argument than the one enunciated by Dr. Gipp. They have broken free from the false etymology advanced by Hislop and realized that historically "Easter" was used to refer to both the Christian festival and the Jewish feast day. These believers reject the traditional defense of "Easter" in Acts 12:4 on pagan grounds, and instead argue that Luke was referring to a Christian celebration as opposed to a pagan or Jewish one. The *KJV Today* article *Easter or Passover in Acts 12:4* is emblematic of this approach.

This position is justified on the grounds that the King James translators rendered *pascha* as "Easter" only one time in Acts 12:4 after the resurrection of Christ. In contrast, before the resurrection or in clear references to the Jewish feast as in I Corinthians 5:7 and Hebrews 11:28 the translators used "Passover" exclusively. Those holding this view maintain that the King James translators reserved "Passover" for references to the Jewish holy day and confined "Easter" to the post-resurrection Christian festival. It is believed by those holding this view that this practice on the part of the King James translators served to settle the use of this terminology for the English language. In other words, from 1611 onward "Passover" would be confined in meaning and usage to the Jewish festival whereas "Easter" would apply exclusively to the Christian commemoration of the resurrection.

While this view is an improvement over the pagan view advanced by Dr. Gipp and others, it still falls short for the following reasons: First, it ignores the clear Jewish context of Acts 12 as laid out in the previous chapter. Second, it does not take into account the clear cross references connecting the "days of unleavened bread" with the Jewish Passover. Third, it makes the dispensational assumption that Peter, James, and John and their followers in Jerusalem were automatically "Christians" after the resurrection in the sense that they were no longer following the Mosaic Law and/or Israel's holy days outlined therein.

Given the totality of the evidence, the conclusion that "Easter" in Acts 12:4 is a reference to the Jewish feast of "Passover" is the soundest conclusion at which one can arrive.

Concluding Thoughts

While we have been very critical of Gipp in this book we cannot let James R. White off the hook either. Recall from Chapter One that White accepted the notion that "Easter" was pagan in origin, anachronistic in usage, and was therefore a mistranslation of *pascha* in Acts 12:4. If White had adequately done his homework, he would have known that etymologically "Easter" was a perfectly acceptable way of referring to the Jewish "Passover." He would have observed the long history of translating the Greek word *pascha* as "Easter" prior to 1611.

These observations regarding the suspect scholarship of White on this point highlight an important overall take away. The anti-King James, pro-Modern Version side of the textual/version debate does not have the market cornered in terms of scholarship as many have falsely assumed. Both sides have fallen prey to the notion that preservation requires *verbatim identicality* of wording which has led them to advance unscriptural notions regarding the doctrine of preservation. One side confines inspiration and inerrancy to the nonexistent original autographs as a means of accounting for variant readings. Meanwhile, the other side ignores the existence of variant readings and insists upon "perfect" or "verbatim" preservation by faith for faith's sake.

In this way, the debate regarding "Easter" in Acts 12:4 is a microcosm of the greater textual debate. King James advocates such as Dr. Gipp claim that the KJB is inerrant. This invites modern version advocates such as Dr. White to prove that the KJB is not inerrant. Thus, we have the current controversy regarding "Easter" in Acts 12:4 in the King James.

Confined by the standard of *verbatim identicality* for "perfect preservation" Dr. Gipp endeavors to defend why the only correct rendering of *pascha* in Acts 12:4 is "Easter." In the mind of Dr. Gipp, there is no possible way that Luke is talking about the Jewish feast of "Passover" in Acts 12 or God would have providentially caused the King James translators to use that word. Therefore, he proceeds to erect a justification for that "exact" word; this is done without even considering that there might be a different way of saying the same thing. Put another way, Gipp is demanding "uniformity of phrasing" in a way that the King James translators did not. Gipp's preconceptions limit the scope of his research before he even commences his investigation. This explains why he ignores the clear cross references in Ezekiel 45:21, Matthew 26:17-18, and Luke 22:1; his explanatory model does not know how to account for these verses.

All of this highlights the need for King James Bible believers to go the extra mile in their study of the text. Those who adopt a pro-King James stance will often cite the archaic forms and manners of speaking as being more precise than modern English in their ability to convey Biblical truth. While I wholeheartedly agree with this notion, it also mandates that additional study is often in order to understand what words meant in the early 17th century when the translation was made. Too often King James advocates ascribe modern usage and meaning to words that did not necessarily mean the same thing in the early 17th century.

This study of "Easter" stands out as a case in point. Modern readers have adopted the false etymology of Hislop and are completely unaware that "Easter" had a long history of being used as a reference to the Jewish "Passover." It was only by looking at pre-1611 English translations, as well as etymological dictionaries, that a clear understanding emerged.

Consider the illustration of the United States Constitution (this is not saying the Constitution was inspired, but only used as an example). Written in the late 18th century, the Constitution, like the King James Bible; contains some archaic language. In our day people argue about the nature of the Constitution. Strict constructionists view the Constitution as a fixed static document that means what it says (literal hermeneutic); whereas loose constructionists view the Constitution as a fluid document that is subject to societal and cultural interpretation (allegorical hermeneutic).

To understand the nature of what is being said, strict constructionists will appeal to what words meant in the late 1700s when the Constitution was drafted as justification for their strict/literal interpretation. Moreover, the Federalist and Anti-Federalist Papers are viewed as commentaries on the "original intent" of America's founders and framers. Strict constructionists will appeal to these sources in order to establish "original intent" or what the Constitution meant at the time of its drafting.

In comparison, King James advocates need to be concerned with the "original intent" of the translators in terms of how they understood and used certain words. A willingness to go the extra mile in terms of research is in order on the part of King James advocates to make sure their understanding of a particular English word corresponds with how the translators understood/used that word. Just as the Federalist and Anti-Federalist Papers, in addition to dictionaries from that time-period aid in establishing the "original intent" of the Constitution; etymological and early 17th century dictionaries, as well as pre-1611 English translations of the *Textus Receptus* aid in establishing the meaning of English words in the early 1600s when the King James Bible was translated.

As in the case of "Easter", King James advocates need to be willing to conduct additional study in order to arrive at sound conclusions.

Bibliography

"Easter" entry in the *Online Etymological Dictionary*. http://www. etymonline.com/index.php?allowed_in_frame=0&search=easter.

"'Easter' or 'Passover' in Acts 12:4?" *King James Version Today*, www. kjvtoday.com/home/easter-or-passover-in-acts-124.

Gipp, Samuel C. *The Answer Book: A Help Book for Christians*. Bible & Literature Missionary Foundation: Shelbyville, TN: 1989.

Hislop, Alexander. *The Two Babylons*. 1853.

Norton, David. *The King James Bible: A Short History from Tyndale to Today*. Cambridge University Press, 2011.

Oxford English Dictionary Online. Oxford University Press. https://www.oed.com

Tegart, Brian. "*Acts 12:4 – Passover and Easter*. http://www.kjv-only.com/acts12_4.html

White, James R. *The King James Only Controversy: Can You Trust Modern Translations?*. Bethany House Publishers: Minneapolis, MN: 1995.

Appendix A

Etymological information on "Easter" provided
by the Oxford English Dictionary

Etymology: Cognate with Old Dutch *ōster-* (in *ōstermānōth* April, lit. 'Easter-month'), Old Saxon *ōstar-* (in *ōstarfrisking* paschal lamb; Middle Low German *ōsteren* , *ōstern* , plural), Old High German *ōstara* (usually in plural *ōstarūn* ; Middle High German *ōster* (usually in plural *ōstern*), German *Ostern* , singular and (now chiefly regional) plural), probably < the same Germanic base as EAST *adv.* (and hence ultimately cognate with Sanskrit *uṣas* , Avestan *ušah-* , ancient Greek (Ionic and Epic) *ἠώς* , (Attic) *ἕως* , classical Latin *aurōra* , all in sense 'dawn'). For alternative (and less likely) etymologies see the references cited below. It is noteworthy that among the Germanic languages the word (as the name for Easter) is restricted to English and German; in other Germanic languages, as indeed in most European languages, the usual word for Easter is derived from the corresponding word for the Jewish Passover; compare PASCH *n.*

Bede (*De Temporum Ratione* 15. 9: see quot. below) derives the word < *Eostre* (a Northumbrian spelling; also *Eastre* in a variant reading), according to him, the name of a goddess whose festival was celebrated by the pagan Anglo-Saxons around the time of the vernal equinox (presumably in origin a goddess of the dawn, as the name is to be derived from the same Germanic base as EAST *adv.*: see above). This explanation is not confirmed by any other source, and the goddess has been suspected by some scholars to be an invention of Bede›s. However, it seems unlikely that Bede would have invented a fictitious pagan festival in order to account for a Christian one. For further discussion and alternative derivations see D. H. Green

Lang. & Hist. Early Germanic World (1998) 351–3, J. Udolph & K. Schäferdieck in *J. Hoops›s Reallexikon der germanischen Altertumskunde* (ed. 2, 2003) XXII. 331–8, and for a parallel development compare YULE *n*. Bede›s etymology comes in a passage explaining the origin of the Old English names of the months:

*a*735 BEDE *De Temporum Ratione* xv Eostur-monath, qui nunc paschalis mensis interpretatur, quondam a dea illorum quae Eostre vocabatur, et cui in illo festa celebrabant, nomen habuit, a cujus nomine nunc paschale tempus cognominant, consueto antiquae observationis vocabulo gaudia novae solemnitatis vocantes.

Compare Old English *Ēastermōnað* April, cognate with or formed similarly to Old Dutch *ōstermānōth* (in a translation from German), Old High German *ōstarmānōd* (Middle High German *ōstermānōt* , German *Ostermonat* , now archaic) < the Germanic base of EASTER *n.1* + the Germanic base of MONTH *n.1*

A borrowing of the Old English word into West Slavonic (during the time of the Anglo-Saxon mission to Germany) perhaps underlies Polabian *jostrǻi* , Lower Sorbian *jatšy* , (regional) *jastry* , Kashubian *jastrë* , all in sense 'Easter'; however, it has been argued that these are rather to be derived from a native base meaning 'clear, bright', and thus (via a connection with the coming of spring) show a parallel development to the Germanic word.

The form of the word in Old English shows much (especially dialectal) variation: in West Saxon usually a weak feminine plural (*Ēastran* ; frequently in form *Ēastron* (also *Ēastrun*), probably reflecting a variant form of the Germanic thematic element: see A. Campbell *Old Eng. Gram.* (1959) §619.1), also occasionally found in the singular (*Ēastre*); an apparently strong feminine plural by-form (*Ēastra*), apparently Mercian, is rarely attested; in Northumbrian usually a strong neuter plural (*Ēostru* , *Ēostro*), also occasionally found in the singular (sometimes apparently invariably as *Ēostro* , sometimes in inflected forms, e.g. genitive *Ēostres*). The combining form *Ēaster* is widely attested.

The β. forms represent Old English *Ēastran* (the form of both the weak feminine plural and the inflected form of the weak feminine singular) and its later reflexes. The forms of some compounds in Middle English and early modern English may reflect compounds of the Old English weak feminine genitive singular or plural (respectively *Ēastran* and *Ēastrena*).

Appendix B

Relevant Dictionary Entries for the Word Easter

"Easter" 1.a. from the *Oxford English Dictionary*

1 The most important and oldest of the festivals of the Christian Church, commemorating the resurrection of Christ and observed annually on the Sunday which follows the first full moon after the vernal equinox. Also (more generally): Easter week or the weekend from Good Friday to Easter Monday, Eastertide. In Old English frequently in *plural*.

> Easter is observed on the first Sunday after the paschal full moon (not the astronomical full moon) which occurs on or after 21 March. The actual date varies according to the calendar used in its calculation.

eOE *Cleopatra Gloss.* in W. G. Stryker *Lat.-Old Eng. Gloss. in MS Cotton Cleopatra A.III* (Ph.D. diss., Stanford Univ.) (1951) 365 *Phase*, eastran.

OE ÆLFRIC *De Temporibus Anni* (Cambr. Gg.3.28) (2009) iv. 84 On sumon geare bið se mona twelf siðon geniwod, fram ðære halgan eastertide oð eft eastron.

OE tr. Bede *Eccl. Hist.* (Cambr. Univ. Libr.) v. xix. 470 Ic þonne nu [eow] openlice andette.., þæt ic ðas tide Eastrena ecelice healdan wille mid ealre minre ðeode.

lOE *Anglo-Saxon Chron.* (Laud) anno 1101 To Cristesmæssan heold se cyng Heanrig his hired on Westmynstre & to Eastran on Winceastre.

a1200 *MS Trin. Cambr.* in R. Morris *Old Eng. Homilies* (1873) 2nd Ser. 101 (*MED*) Þe þre dage biforen estre [ben] cleped swidages.

*c*1275 (*?a*1200)   Laȝamon *Brut* (Calig.) (1978) l. 9230   He ferde to Lunden. He wes þere an Æstre.

*c*1300 *St. Brendan* (Harl.) l. 151 in C. Horstmann *Early S.-Eng. Legendary* (1887) 224   Þer ȝe schulle þis ester beo, & þis wit-sonedai also.

*a*1325 (*c*1250)   *Gen. & Exod.* (1968) l. 3289   Ðor-of in esterne be we wunen Seuene siðes to funt cumen.

1389   in J. T. Smith & L. T. Smith *Eng. Gilds* (1870) 35   Þe soneday fourtnythe after esterne.

1440   *Promptorium Parvulorum* (Harl. 221) 143/2   Eesterne, *Pascha*.

*a*1450 *St. Edith* (Faust.) (1883) l. 3140   Þis miracle was þus..y-do, In þe astere nexste after hurre body-dyenge.

1480   W. Caxton *Chron. Eng.* ccxxxiii. 254   The clergye..wold not graunte vnto Estre next comyng.

1530   *Myroure Oure Ladye* (Fawkes) (1873) ii. 278   From passyon sonday tyl Esterne.

1593   R. Hooker *Of Lawes Eccl. Politie* iv. xi. 194   Keeping the feast of Easter on the same day the Iewes kept theirs.

1655   T. Fuller *Church-hist. Brit.* ii. 55   The Spring-time, wherein the Feast of Easter..was celebrated.

1680   J. Dryden *Kind Keeper* iv. i. 39   He made me keep Lent last year till Whitsontide, and out-fac'd me with Oaths, it was but Easter.

*a*1712   G. Martine *Reliquiæ Divi Andreae* (1797) 188   The senȝie mercat.. beginning the second week after Easter.

1782   J. Priestley *Hist. Corruptions Christianity* II. viii. 129   The first.. festival..that was observed..was Easter.

1838   W. Howitt *Rural Life Eng.* II. iii. iv. 166   Easter was the great festival of the church.

1863   G. Meredith *Let.* 15 Apr. (1970) I. 199   By the way, my darling little man came home at Easter.

1916   'Taffrail' *Pincher Martin* viii. 142   Most of the younger men were past caring whether it was Christmas or Easter.

1954   *Los Angeles Times* 12 Apr. ii. 10/4   A bowlful of pysanky, blessed at Easter, guards a Ukrainian home against lightning and fire.

1993   *Independent* 22 Feb. 10/4   I used to visit her at Easter and the summer hols, and cried buckets when I left her.

2006   *St James› Parish Mag.* (Blackburn) Apr. 9   The sacrifice of Jesus Christ upon the cross, enfolded in the glory of Easter.

"Easter" 2. from the *Oxford English Dictionary*

2. = PASSOVER *n.* 1. Now only in *Jewish Easter* or with other contextual indication [See Appendix C for the OED's definition of Passover n. 1.].

OE   *Blickling Homilies* 67   Hælend cwom syx dagum ær Iudea eastrum, to Bethania.

OE   *West Saxon Gospels: Mark* (Corpus Cambr.) xiv. 1   Soþlice þa æfter twam dagum wæron eastron.

*a*1398   J. TREVISA tr. Bartholomaeus Anglicus *De Proprietatibus Rerum* (BL Add. 27944) (1975) I. ix. xxxi. 546   Ester hatte *pascha* in grewe..and is iclepid in ebrewe *phase*, þat is 'passinge oþir passage'.

*c*1450 (*c*1400)   *Bk. Vices & Virtues* (Huntington) (1942) 131 (*MED*)   Wiþ grete desire I haue desired þis Eestren, þat is þis Paske.

1535   *Bible* (Coverdale) Ezek. xlv. 21   Vpon ye xiiij. daye of the first moneth ye shal kepe Easter.

1563   *2nd Tome Homelyes* Whitsunday i, in J. Griffiths *Two Bks. Homilies* (1859) ii. 453   Easter, a great, and solemne feast among the Iewes.

1611   *Bible* (King James) Acts xii. 4   Intending after Easter to bring him foorth.

1662   P. GUNNING *Paschal or Lent-Fast* 37   S. Iohn and S. Philip finding it usefull..to observe the Christian Easter on the same day with the Jewish Easter.

1792   J. DOUGLAS *Disc. Infl. Christian Relig.* xii. 213   The catastrophe took place at the celebration of Easter, when the Jews had flocked to the city from the distant regions of the empire.

1812   *Port Folio* Sept. 297   An extract from two Hebrew works on the Jewish easter.

1883   J. L. MEAGHER *Festal Year* viii. 281   The Jews held their Easter on the fourteenth moon of the month of March.

1934 *Times* 24 Dec. 9/6 During the 14 years from A.D. 20 to 33 the only year in which the Jewish Easter (15 Nisan) fell on a Friday was the year 27.

1973 *Adolescent Psychiatry* **3** 60 Hence, the English name Passover for the Jewish Easter.

2004 J. LLOYD tr. J. Pérez *Spanish Inquisition* 19 They..ceased all activities on the day of the sabbath, recited Jewish prayers, celebrated Jewish Easter and other festivals.

Ēster from the *Middle English Dictionary*

ēster(n n.

Forms: ēster(n n. Also ester, estre(n, aster(n, yestre.

Etymology: OE ēaster (pl. ēastro) and ēastre (pl. eastran, -on); ēaster-dæg, ēaster-tīd, etc.

Definitions (Senses and Subsenses)

1.

The church festival of Easter; Easter Sunday; the Easter season;-- usually without article.

2.

The Jewish Passover.

"Easter" from *American Dictionary of the English Language* (1828)

E'ASTER, noun

A festival of the Christian church observed in commemoration of our Savior's resurrection. It answers to the pascha or passover of the Hebrews, and most nations still give it this name, pascha, pask, paque.

Appendix C

Oxford English Dictionary entry for "Passover"

I. Senses relating to the Jewish festival.

1.

a. The major Jewish spring festival which commemorates the liberation of the People of Israel from Egyptian bondage, lasting seven days (in Israel) or eight days (in the Diaspora) from the 15th day of Nisan. Cf. PESACH *n.*

1530 *Bible (*Tyndale*)* Exod. xii. f. xviiiv And ye shall eate it in haste, for it is the Lordes passeouer.

1535 *Bible (*Coverdale*)* Exod. xii. 43 This is the maner of the kepynge of Passeouer.

1563 G. HAY *Confut. Abbote of Cosraguels Masse* 62 If the eating [of the Pascal lamb] had bene omitted..the whole action of the Pasouer wes but a sacrifice.

1608 *Dispute Question of Kneeling* 49 The circumstance of the Evening, and of the infermentation belonged peculiarly to the feast of the Passover, and of the unleavened bread.

1662 W. GURNALL *Christian in Armour: 3rd Pt.* 687 Baptism is clearer than Circumcision, Lords Supper than Passeover.

1725 D. COTES tr. L. E. Du Pin *New Eccl. Hist. 17th Cent.* I. v. 67 This Custom of bidding the Passover on the Day of the Epiphany.

1797 *Encycl. Brit.* XIV. 17/2 The modern Jews observe in general the same ceremonies that were practised by their ancestors, in the celebration of the passover.

1840   *Penny Cycl.* XVII. 304   *Passover*..also called the feast of unleavened bread.

1893   J. A. BROADUS *Harm. Gospels* 243   The Bi-paschal theory makes the time of the public life of Jesus one year, allowing only two Passovers to the Gospel of John.

1947   *Amer. Sociol. Rev.* 12 195/2   He was introduced to matzoth when a Jewish woman brought some to his family on Passover.

1963   *Jrnl. Afr. Hist.* 4 337   The only restriction of which the Jews complained was the prohibition of exhibiting the Tora in public at Passover.

2002   *Vanity Fair* (N.Y.) Jan. 150/2   The Palestinian leader called to congratulate him on the birth of twin grandsons and to wish him a happy Passover.

Appendix D

Old Testament Occurrences

	Tyndale (1530 Pen.)	Coverdale (1535)	Matthews (1537)	Great (1539)	Geneva (1560)	Bishops (1568)	KJB (1611)
Ex. 12:11	passeouer	passeouer	passeouer	passeouer	passeouer	passeouer	passeouer
Ex. 12:21	passeouer	passeouer	passeouer	passeouer	passeouer	passeouer	passeouer
Ex. 12:27	passeouer	passeouer	passeouer	passeouer	passeouer	passeouer	passeouer
Ex. 12:43	passeouer	passeouer	passeouer	passeouer	passeouer	passeouer	passeouer
Ex. 12:48	passeouer	passeouer	passeouer	passeouer	passeouer	passeouer	passeouer
Ex. 34:25	passeouer	*Easter*	passeouer	passeouer	passeouer	passeouer	passeouer
Lev. 23:5	passeouer	*Easter*	passeouer	passeouer	passeouer	passeouer	passeouer
Num. 9:2	passeouer	*Easter*	passeouer	passeouer	passeouer	passeouer	passeouer
Num. 9:4	passeouer	*Easter*	passeouer	passeouer	passeouer	passeouer	passeouer

	Tyndale (1530 Pen.)	Coverdale (1535)	Matthews (1537)	Great (1539)	Geneva (1560)	Bishops (1568)	KJB (1611)
Num. 9:5	passeouer	*Easter*	passeouer	passeouer	passeouer	passeouer	passeouer
Num. 9:6	passeouer	*Easter*	passeouer	passeouer	passeouer	passeouer	passeouer
Num. 9:10	passeouer	*Easter*	passeouer	passeouer	passeouer	passeouer	passeouer
Num. 9:12	passeouer	*Easter*	passeouer	passeouer	passeouer	passeouer	passeouer
Num. 9:13	passeouer	*Easter*	passeouer	passeouer	passeouer	passeouer	passeouer
Num. 9:14	passeouer (2x)	*Easter* (2x)	passeouer (2x)	passeouer (2x)	passeouer (2x)	passeouer (2x)	passeouer (2x)
Num. 28:16	passeouer	*Easter*	passeouer	passeouer	passeouer	passeouer	passeouer
Num. 33:3	passeouer	*Easter*	passeouer	passeouer	passeouer	passeouer	passeouer
Due. 16:1	passeouer	*Easter*	passeouer	passeouer	passeouer	passeouer	passeouer
Due. 16:2	passeouer	*Easter*	passeouer	passeouer	passeouer	passeouer	passeouer
Due. 16:5	passeouer	*Easter*	passeouer	passeouer	passeouer	passeouer	passeouer
Due. 16:6	passeouer	*Easter*	passeouer	passeouer	passeouer	passeouer	passeouer

	Tyndale (1530 Pen.)	Coverdale (1535)	Matthews (1537)	Great (1539)	Geneva (1560)	Bishops (1568)	KJB (1611)
Josh. 5:10		Easter	passeouer	passeouer	passeouer	passeouer	passeouer
Josh. 5:11		Easter	passeouer	passeouer	passeouer	passeouer	passeouer
III Kg. 23:21		Easter	passeouer	passeouer	passeouer	passeouer	passeouer
II Kg. 23:22		Easter	passeouer	passeouer	passeouer	passeouer	passeouer
III Kg. 23:23		Easter	passeouer	passeouer	passeouer	passeouer	passeouer
II Ch. 30:1		Easter	passeouer	passeouer	passeouer	passeouer	passeouer
II Ch. 30:2		passeouer	passeouer	passeouer	passeouer	passeouer	passeouer
II Ch. 30:5		passeouer	passeouer	passeouer	passeouer	passeouer	passeouer
II Ch. 30:15		passeouer	passeouer	passeouer	passeouer	passeouer	passeouer
II Ch. 30:18		Easter lambe	passeouer	passeouer	passeouer	passeouer	passeouer
II Ch. 35:1		passeouer	passeouer	passeouer	passeouer	passeouer	passeouer
II Ch. 35:6		passeouer	passeouer	passeouer		passeouer	passeouer

	Tyndale (1530 Pen.)	Coverdale (1535)	Matthews (1537)	Great (1539)	Geneva (1560)	Bishops (1568)	KJB (1611)
II Ch. 35:7		passeouer	passeouer	passeouer	passeouer	passeouer	passeouer
II Ch. 35:8		passeouer	passeouer	passeouer	passeouer	passeouer	passeouer
II Ch. 35:9		passeouer	passeouer	passeouer	passeouer	passeouer	passeouer
II Ch. 35:11		passeouer	passeouer	passeouer	passeouer	passeouer	passeouer
II Ch. 35:13		passeouer	passeouer	passeouer	passeouer	passeouer	passeouer
II Ch. 35:16		passeouer	passeouer	passeouer	passeouer	passeouer	passeouer
II Ch. 35:17		passeouer	passeouer	passeouer	passeouer	passeouer	passeouer
II Ch. 35:18		passeouer	passeouer	passeouer	passeouer	passeouer	passeouer
II Ch. 35:19		passeouer	passeouer	passeouer	passeouer	passeouer	passeouer
Ezra 6:19		passeouer	passeouer	passeouer	passeouer	passeouer	passeouer
Ezra 6:20		passeouer	passeouer	passeouer	passeouer	passeouer	passeouer
Ezk. 45:21		*Easter*	*Easter*	*easter*	passeouer	passeouer	passeouer

Chart of New Testament Occurrences – Part 1

	WestSaxon (990 Gos.)	WestSaxon (1175 Gos.)	Wycliffe (1382–1395)	Luther (1522 NT)	Tyndale (1526 NT)	Coverdale (1535)
Matt. 26:2	eastre	eastre	pask	Ostern	ester	Easter
Matt. 26:17	eastron	eastren	paske	Osterlamm	paschall	Easter
Matt. 26:18	eastro	eastre	paske	Ostern	ester	Easter
Matt. 26:19	easter-penunga	eastren-peg-nunge	paske	Osterlamm	esterlambe	Easter lambe
Mark 14:1	eastron	eastren	Pask	Ostern	ester	Easter
Mark 14:12	eastron eastron	eastren eastren	pask pask	Osterlamm Osterlamm	pascall lambe ester lambe	Easter lambe Easter labe
Mark 14:14	eastron	eastren	pask	Osterlamm	ester lambe	Easter labe
Mark 14:16	eastron	eastren	pask	Osterlamm	ester lambe	Easter lambe
Luke 2:41	easter-dæges	eastre daiges	pask	Osterfest	feeste of ester	feast of Easter
Luke 22:1	eastre	eastre	pask	Ostern	ester	Easter

	WestSaxon (990 Gos.)	WestSaxon (1175 Gos.)	Wycliffe (1382–1395)	Luther (1522 NT)	Tyndale (1526 NT)	Coverdale (1535)
Luke 22:7	eastron	eastren	pask	Osterlamm	esterlambe	Easter lambe
Luke 22:8	eastron	eastren	pask	Osterlamm	ester lambe	Easter lambe
Luke 22:11	eastron	eastren	pask	Osterlamm	ester lambe	Easter labe
Luke 22:13	eastrun	eastren	pask	Osterlamm	ester lambe	Easter lambe
Luke 22:15	eastron	eastren	pask	Osterlamm	ester lambe	Easter labe
John 2:13	eastron	eastron	pask	Ostern	ester	Easter
John 2:23	eastron	eastron	pask	Ostern	ester	Easter
John 6:4	eastron	eastren	pask	Ostern	ester	Easter
John 11:55	eastron eastron	eastre eastran	pask pask	Ostern Ostern	ester ester	Easter Easter
John 12:1	eastron	eastren	pask	Ostern	ester	Easter
John 13:1	esterfreols	easter	pask	Ostern	ester	Easter
John 18:28	eastron	eastran	pask	Ostern	paschal lambe	pascal lambe

	WestSaxon (990 Gos.)	WestSaxon (1175 Gos.)	Wycliffe (1382-1395)	Luther (1522 NT)	Tyndale (1526 NT)	Coverdale (1535)
John 18:39	*eastron*	*eastren*	pask	*Ostern*	*ester*	Easter
John 19:14	*eastra*	*eastre*	pask	*Ostern*	*ester*	*Easter*
Acts 12:4	–	–	pask	*Ostern*	*ester*	*Easter*
I Cor. 5:7	–	–	pask	*Osterlamm*	*esterlambe*	*Easter lambe*
Heb. 11:28	–	–	pask	*Ostern*	*ester*	*Easter*
Totals	The WestSaxon Gospels of 990 use some form of "Easter" all 26 times the Jewish Passover is referenced in the Gospels.	The WestSaxon Gospels of 1175 use some form of "Easter" all 26 times the Jewish Passover is referenced in the Gospels.	Wycliffe transliterated the Latin equivalent of *pascha* of 29 times that it occurs in the New Testament	Luther used some form of *"Ostern"* all 29 times that *pascha* was found in the *TR*.	Tyndale used "paschal" or "paschal lamb" 3 different times and some form of "Easter" the remaining 26 times.	Coverdale used the expression "paschal lambe" 1 time and some form of "Easter" the remaining 28 times.

Chart of New Testament Occurrences – Part 2

	Matthews (1537)	Great (1539)	Geneva NT (1557)	Geneva (1560)	Bishops (1568)	KJB (1611)
Matt. 26:2	easter	Easter	Easter	Passeouer	Passouer	passover
Matt. 26:17	paschall	passeouer	passeouer	Passeouer	Passouer	passover
Matt. 26:18	easter	Easter	Easter	Passeouer	Passouer	passover
Matt. 26:19	easter lambe	passeouer	passeouer	Passeouer	Passouer	passover
Mark 14:1	easter	Easter	Easter	Passeouer	Passouer	passover
Mark 14:12	pascall lambe / easter lambe	Passeouer / Passeouer	Paschal lambe / Easter lambe	Passeouer / Passeouer	Passouer / Passouer	passover / passover
Mark 14:14	easter lambe	passeouer	Easter lambe	Passeouer	Passouer	passover
Mark 14:16	easter lambe	Passeouer	Easter lambe	Passeouer	Passouer	passover
Luke 2:41	feaste of easter	feaste of easter	feast of Easter	feast of the Passeouer	feast of ye Passouer	Feast of the passover
Luke 22:1	easter	Easter	Easter	Passeouer	Passouer	Passover

	Matthews (1537)	Great (1539)	Geneva NT (1557)	Geneva (1560)	Bishops (1568)	KJB (1611)
Luke 22:7	*easterlambe*	Passeouer	Passeouer	Passeouer	Passeouer	passover
Luke 22:8	*easterlambe*	Passeouer	*Easter lambe*	Passeouer	Passeouer	passover
Luke 22:11	*easterlambe*	Passeouer	*Easter lambe*	Passeouer	Passeouer	passover
Luke 22:13	*easterlambe*	Passeouer	*Easter lambe*	Passeouer	Passeouer	Passover
Luke 22:15	*easterlambe*	Passeouer	*Easter lambe*	Passeouer	Passeouer	passover
John 2:13	*easter*	ester	*Easter*	Passeouer	Passeouer	passover
John 2:23	*easter*	Easter	*Easter*	Passeouer	Passeouer	passover
John 6:4	*easter*	easter	*Easter*	Passeouer	Passeouer	passover
John 11:55	*Easter* *Easter*	Easter Easter	*Easter* *Easter*	Passeouer Passeouer	*Easter* *Easter*	passover passover
John 12:1	*Easter*	Easter	*Easter*	Passeouer	Passeouer	passover
John 13:1	*Easter*	Easter	*Easter*	Passeouer	Passeouer	passover
John 18:28	paschal lambe	Passeouer	Paschal lambe	Passeouer	Passeouer	passover

	Matthews (1537)	Great (1539)	Geneva NT (1557)	Geneva (1560)	Bishops (1568)	KJB (1611)
John 18:39	*Easter*	*Easter*	*Easter*	Passeouer	Passeouer	passover
John 19:14	*easter*	*easter*	*Easter*	Passeouer	Passeouer	passover
Acts 12:4	*Easter*	*Ester*	*Easter*	Passeouer	*Easter*	*Easter*
I Cor. 5:7	*easterlambe*	passeouer	*Easter lambe*	Passeouer	Pasouer	passover
Heb. 11:28	*Easter*	passeouer	*Easter lambe*	Passeouer	Passouer	passover
Totals	Matthews followed Tyndale in using a form of "paschal" 3 times and some form of "Easter" 26 times.	The Great Bible demonstrates the most diversity. 15 times some form of "Easter" is used whereas 14 times the word "Passover" is used.	The Geneva NT of 1557 only used the word "Passover" 3 times and a form of "Paschal" 2 times. The remaining 24 occurrences of *pascha* were rendered as some form of "Easter."	The complete Geneva Bible of 1560 uniformly uses the word "Passover" all 29 times that *pascha* is found in the *TR*.	The Bishops Bible contains the word "Easter" three times. Twice in Jhn. 11:55 and once in Acts 12:4. The remaining 26 occurrences of *pascha* are rendered "Passover" in English.	The KJB retains the word "Easter" in only verse, Acts 12:4. Every other time *pascha* occurs in the text it is translated as "Passover" by the King James translators.

OTHER WORKS BY THE AUTHOR

Available at www.DispensationalPublishing.com

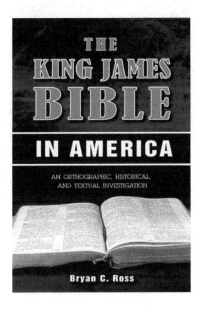

The King James Bible in America: An Orthographic, Historical, and Textual Investigation

Do changes of spelling or slight differences of wording create a corrupt version of the Bible? This position of "verbatim identicality" is held by many users of the King James Bible, and is thoughtfully challenged by a KJB user. Readers will gain a history of the KJB in America, as well as knowledge of some important words which seem strange to the modern American eye.

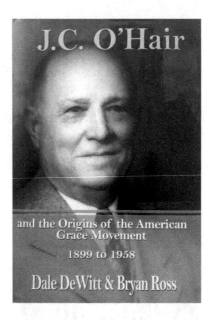

J.C. O'Hair and the Origins of the American Grace Movement.

By Dale DeWitt and Bryan Ross

When J.C. O'Hair died in January of 1958, he received well-deserved honors, appreciation, and affectionate regard in memoirs and sermons. Over the course of his ministry, he endeared himself to thousands, not by design but because of who he was; a jovial, affirming personality, a man of leadership, preaching, and teaching charisma. O'Hair's most important insight was a line of reasoning for his placement of Acts' transition, recognizing Israel, the law, and the available Messianic kingdom at the beginning of the book with a subsequent and momentous changeover to grace and the free inclusion of the Gentiles for the remainder of the book.

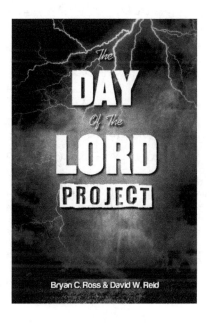

The Day of the Lord Project

Bryan Ross and David Reid

Pastors Bryan Ross and David Reid provide a thorough understanding of the Day of the Lord. These two Bible teachers accurately identify the nature and timing of the day of the Lord in Scripture. In addition, specific attention is given to the Day of Christ and how this uniquely Pauline revelation relates to the day of the Lord in prophecy.

...we believe on him that raised up Jesus our Lord from the dead; who was delivered for our offences, + was raised for our justification. Rom.

"Being justified freely by his grace through the redemption that is in Christ Jesus": whom God hath set forth to be a propitiation through faith in his blood, to declare his righteousness for the remission of sins that are past... just, + the justifier of him "w/ believeth in Jesus Rom 3:24-26

Much more then, being now justified by his blood, we shall be saved from wrath through him. For if when we were enemies, we were reconciled to God by the death of his Son... we shall be saved by his life. Rom. 5:9-10

Freely - justified - w/ believeth in Jesus
        Ye have received
    Rev. Water of life
        Isaiah - he that hath no money

Dispensational Publishing House is striving to become the go-to source for Bible-based materials from the dispensational perspective.

Our goal is to provide high-quality doctrinal and worldview resources that make dispensational theology accessible to people at all levels of understanding.

Visit our blog regularly to read informative articles from both known and new writers.

And please let us know how we can better serve you.

Dispensational Publishing House, Inc.
PO Box 3181
Taos, NM 87571

Call us toll free 844-321-4202

www.DispensationalPublishing.com

Rom

Gospel of Christ: power of God unto salvation
to everyone that believeth. 1:16

. all under sin - None righteous 8:9-10
. every mouth may be stopped, + all the world may
become guilty before God 3:19

Righteousness of God w/is by faith of Jesus Christ
unto all + upon all them that believe.

— Just + the justifier of him w/ believeth in Jesus
Rom 3:26
if we believe on him that raised up Jesus our
Lord from the dead; who was delivered for our
offenses, + was raised again for our justification. Rom 4 24-25

— we were enemies, we were reconciled to God
by the death of his Son. Rom 5:9-10

(ambassador for Christ

2 Cor 4 Lest the light of the g. gospel of Christ
... glory of God in the face of Jesus
Christ. — Always delivered unto death for
Jesus' sake. He w/ raised up Jesus
shall raise up also by Jesus
(John)

Ye know neither me nor the Father, if ye had known me
If God were your Father ye would love me
— proceedeth forth.

CPSIA information can be obtained
at www.ICGtesting.com
Printed in the USA
LVHW080141230620
658764LV00017B/282

Seeth me

seen/noted

9 781945 774447